SONGS OF DESERT WINDS

Songs of
Desert Winds

WILLIAM DUNN

Copyright © 2025 William Dunn

All rights reserved.

No part of this book may be reproduced, stored in a retrieval system, or transmitted in any form, or by any means, electronic, mechanical, photocopying, or otherwise, without the prior written permission of the publisher, except by a reviewer, who may quote brief passages in a review.

Os Justi Press
P.O. Box 21814
Lincoln, NE 68542
www.osjustipress.com

Send inquiries to
info@osjustipress.com

ISBN 978-1-965303-37-5 (paperback)
ISBN 978-1-965303-38-2 (hardcover)

Layout by Michael Schrauzer
Cover by Julian Kwasniewski
Painting on cover by
Maynard Dixon (1875-1946)

In memoriam Leslie Kaufmann
A sacred star of light

CONTENTS

Preface   xiii

I   MOTES OF MORTALITY   1

The Watchmaker   3
The Time of Solitude   4
Polyphemus   5
Song of the Mountain Wind   6
The Old Storage Shed   7
Ruins in a Desert   8
The Moth   9
The Seagull   10
The Modern Astronomer   11
"Go Figure"   12
The Light of Childhood   13
You'll Think of Me As Living   14
The Kite   15
The Jingling of the Bells   16
The Half-Moon   17
Black Crow   18
Birds and Bullets   19
The Gravedigger   20
Memento Mori   21
The Geode   22
The Nordic Funeral Pyre   23
The Firefly   24
The Empty Coffin   25
Diggers of Wells   26
The Diamond and the Raft   27
Cities of Gold   28
The Cemetery Tree   30
Cherubim Sword   31
Black Flowers   32
Hecate   33
Hurricane Land   34
Looking into the Sea   35
The Cracking of the Round Table   36

II VESTIGES OF ETERNITY 37
   Morning Teacup 39
   The First Mineral 40
   Ruins on a Sea Cliff in Ireland 41
   Hy-Brasil 42
   Mists of Ireland 43
   Rembrandt 44
   Prayer for a Dying Girl 45
   Forest Sanctuary 46
   On the Death of an Infant 47
   Waterfalls 48
   The Popular Press 49
   Beside the Stream 50
   Ancestors 51
   Acrobats 52
   The Call of Anaxagoras 53
   Walk Along the Beach 54

III MODERNITY'S NEGATION 55
   Married Lesbians 57
   "To which the year did summon us
      in his delightful round" 58
   The Anadarko 59
   Culture of Death 60
   Strange Confusion 61
   Industrialists 61
   Medieval Angel 61
   The Archaeologist's Dilemma 62
   Of Jets and Longships 63
   The News Cycle 64
   Distinctions 65
   Children's Hands 66
   Prescience 67
   Fiddlesticks! 67
   Arachne 68
   Declaration of Independence 69
   Our Grey Confusion 70

  The Joker and His Minions 71
  A Democrat Meets a Demagogue 72
  The Demon Beggar 73
  Turn Away 74
  Eternity's on the Verge 75
  Mayday, Mayday 76

IV REDEMPTION'S MYSTERY 77
  Renunciation 79
  The Wheel 80
  Verbum Efficit 81
  The Woods of Bethlehem 82
  Vietnam 83
  Mount Athos 84
  The Ancient Choir 85
  St. Thérèse in the Pantheon 86
  Thorns and Diamonds 87
  The Mayfly 88
  Blind Dust 89
  The mass of Mass... 90
  Heretic's Dilemma 91
  On the Shedding of Blood 92
  In the Fullness of Time 93
  An Innocent Cross 93
  Eden and Atlantis 94
  Egyptian Hieroglyphs 95
  Our Passing 96
  Wonder's Depths 97
  The Spell of Heraclitus 98
  Divine Tornado 99
  An Arthurian Mystery 100
  The Bell 101
  Mary of the Circling Stars 102
  Lady of the Sea 103
  Final Breath 104

V   THE SEASONS' WHEEL   105
    Tree Frog   107
    The Church Door   108
    Forest in Rain   109
    Fireworks   110
    The Spectral Horseman   111
    Harvest of the Leaves   112
    The Celtic Mystery   113
    Leaves in the Night   114
    Children in Autumn   115
    Autumn's the Season   116
    Autumn Clouds   117
    The Acorn Tree   118
    Abandoned Train Tracks   119
    The Winter of Us All   120
    Falling Snow   121
    Winter Bridge   122
    The Dying of the Year   123
    The Ancient Hermit   124
    Falling Snows   125
    Christmas MMXX   126
    Winter's Curse   127
    A Christmas Poem   128
    Blossoms in the Briars   129
    The Swallow   130
    The Red Honeysuckle   131
    Dust of Lent   132
    Child of Spring   133
    Sakura   134
    Climbing the Maple Tree   135

About the Author   137

PREFACE

Of all forms of writing, poetry seems most eternal, since it involves the deepest communion with the Muse. I discovered in my youth the many defenders of traditional prosody, of the deepest music of traditional poetry with its meter and rhyme. My poetry is rooted in the mysteries of the Catholic Faith. I have expressed my soul in my poems, and my soul's depths are Catholic depths, reaching into the tradition of the Desert Fathers of the most ancient desert. Nevertheless, I believe these pages will be accessible to all, as they deal again and again with what is perennial, mortal, immortal. I write my poems in freedom of spirit. Chopin, Plato, Aristotle, the Desert Fathers, St. Thomas Aquinas—their spirit is in all my poetry, along with noblest Beethoven, and others who have haunted my spirit throughout this fading world.

Some of the poems included in this collection were first published in the *St. Austin Review* (*StAR*). My thanks to Joseph Pearce for his support and for the permission to republish them here.

I

Motes of Mortality

THE WATCHMAKER

A watchmaker in a jeweler's shop
Revives a watch from forgotten years
Where a century past, an ancient crop
Made a harvest of mortal hopes and fears

He revives the tick of its deepest heart
Which turns the wheels of our cosmic orbs
Where dust of wheat still plays its part
As eternity all time absorbs

For the mainspring is the main thing
That turns the plow at the furrows' end
Where the clockwork birds in stations sing
Where reddening feathers spring greetings send

For the tick-tock of the cuckoo clock
Like voodoo drums of Congo Square
Shall sound alarums of the ancient knock
Whose second coming men must beware

For the tick is followed by the tock's delay
Where all men feast like those asleep
But the watchmaker will not stay away
When time's appointment he must keep

THE TIME OF SOLITUDE

We must learn to drink from rivers of solitude
That echo beneath the earth in oldest caverns
Glimmering still in our human imagination
Where the colder winds blow free

Of Adam's curse
Till caught in the clutch of God.

POLYPHEMUS

Great Cyclops, with your single circling eye,
Polyphemus, with your many numbering songs,
Tell us why the changeling man was born to cry
In countless breaking waves of mortal wrongs.

Tell us of the webs that cross your seas
In patterns weaved by fallen forest ships,
And tell us of that center no man sees,
Where wave on wave the life of mankind slips.

Tell us of the ploughs that cross your earth,
Where all the waving grains are born to die,
And tell us of those signatures of dearth
Where all the scattered graves of mankind lie.

Tell us of the weaver's cosmic web
Where endless waves still cross the changeless warp,
Where undulating time must one day ebb
In the stillness of the sacred golden cup.

SONG OF THE MOUNTAIN WIND

There is a language of the mountain wind
Piercing pine needles that echo mournful peaks
For those below the message cannot send
Drowned in sunsets of our crimson streaks
Fairy blossoms across spring fields strewn
The solemn wind cannot convey
For the marble sculptor whose whitest beauty's hewn
The iron wind could never stray
But for the wrinkled one on his ivory cane
The wind will whisper its ancient tune
Of springs still green in an endless rain
And whispering sands 'cross mankind's desert dune

THE OLD STORAGE SHED

Haunted is my memory
Of a shed within the hill;
Its roof was made of grass
And all within was still.

Haunted is my memory
Of childhood's startling ray
Which ancient morning sun
Still casts through parting day.

On the floor of Adam's dust
There lay the solemn bones
Of a coiled serpent of the past
When I a child stood alone.

Long I stood within that shed
While childhood passed me by
Within the weight of the morning sun
That crushed the serpent and his lie.

RUINS IN A DESERT

Through the ruins of a house of the crackling plaster
That housed the lamps of the white alabaster
One sees through a hole where the window would glisten
The desert where faded spirits would listen

To music which spoke through the feathery curtain
Where tales of the wells were always most certain
And always ran dry when the sands were a whisper
In the blue of the twilight of the ceaseless vesper

And then the far mountain was once again kneeling
Beneath the bright stars all silently wheeling
Absorbing our days so fitfully fading
Where living and dead were endlessly trading

THE MOTH

On the windowpane the nightly moth
Has spread its wings in electric light,
While amber words of mind are wrought
In the lamp of thought's delight.

Its wings of grey and black and white
That captured night and time and space
Are ash of ancient firelight
That crackled before a human face.

THE SEAGULL

Be not the bird above the wrinkling sea
Whose iron waves stretch past infinity,
Cast away your whispering wings of white
Echoing in the pine-wrapped mountain's height,
Strive not for solemn poet's speech
Like cry of gull above our trackless beach
Where seldom mortal soul is found,
When fleeting mortals make their only round
In concrete cities where their shadows play,
Where fading sea-light cannot stay.
Be not the bird that sees all fading light
When iron waves stretch out to endless night.

THE MODERN ASTRONOMER

How many prophets have addressed the sun
Standing like madmen towards desert's empty breath
Marking the shadow where morning had begun
Till eagle's fading cry through twilight's death

And then were stars above the wrinkled sea
Where earth still spun through cold galactic night
Which a trillion galaxies will never see
Plunging through all voids of vanishings of light

For our sun which wheels around the Milky Way
Will through its spinning atoms slowly burn
Consuming itself, the sum that some will pay
As dancing planets towards cold oblivion turn

"GO FIGURE"

"Go figure." It's an odd saying—
Conjures images of the bronze spears slaying
In days of the ancient abacus,
And lines in sands, and oceans beside us.
But a figure is no treasure, so they say,
Since numbers calculate man's dismay,
Assaying debt, and counting total years
Which cannot cypher mortal fears
Or twigs that crisscross dying winter sun
In creaking trees, when life had just begun,
When brazen serpent held against the sky
Was only medicine of mortals doomed to die,
When ocean waves still whispered cross the shore
To measure numbered minutes never more
Before returning to that ancient Deep
Where stars alone can reckon the cosmic Keep.

THE LIGHT OF CHILDHOOD

If you would embrace the fading sun
Then first retrace your childhood's path,
Through worlds of woods of shadows spun
Where all man's shadows memory hath.

If you would retrace your life begun
Then first uproot your life's untruth,
Untangle knots of shadows spun
In fading words of a child's truth.

YOU'LL THINK OF ME AS LIVING

You'll think of me as living
With eyes so strangely blue,
Just like the sky above us
That looks on me and you

A friend sat there beside me
When we were two plus two
Like every life that's just begun,
That's just like me and you

But I died a murder victim
Where an ancient memory grew
And my friend sits still beside me
Where death is still too new

And so he writes with numbered words
Beneath a sky of blue
Where the deep is still above us
And mortal words too few

THE KITE

Paperwhite still flies our human kite
To fill the skies with blanched and mortal fright
As it mimics color of the nightly star
That steers its course through deepest dark afar
For how could one traverse such endless deep
But held to strings that can't forever keep,
Which hold together with all windswept dust
While drift of leaves too soon shall mold and must,
Which stirs the stars to turn to fading light
Of broken string of childhood's fading kite

THE JINGLING OF THE BELLS

The pregnant poppies filled with crimson blood
Will give birth to imagination's flood
Where what is real is what is most surreal
Where wounded cosmos will in deserts steel
In cactus tombs against a spectral sky
Where every voice still cries its question why
As stars give answer in their falling dust
Which glitters in the automotive rust
In rainbow sheens across an oily pool
Like shadows in the deserts of the fool
Whose ancient bells still jangle in his hood
As he questions drifting atoms men call good
As he checkmates within his feathered flood
The drift of stars composed of Adam's blood
Where still he calls where Adam's atoms grind
To help the men of dust their spirits find

THE HALF-MOON

Only the half-moon in the deepest night
Can speak to soul in darkest blight
As fissure rends the soul of ancient man
When lemmings off the cliff in shadows ran

Nuclear fission, or fusion, who cares
When nuclear shadows sell all antique wares
When electron skeletons spell out night
When Adam turned from God in fright

In ghostly electrons, mortal fray
To send out ancient deadly spray
We cannot look in deathly fusion sun
Or futile life in ancient time begun

We see into the ancient mystery
Where only death sets mortals free
In mushroom bomb of great aplomb
Where death of mortal speech is never long

BLACK CROW

Black crow on barren branch of time
You mock the ancient scarecrow's crime
Who conjures ghosts from dusty fields
Where straw-filled shirt your hollowness wields
To slay the hearts of fading gold
Which man's forgotten mysteries told
Before all crimson leaves will spill
Where gaping earth must take its fill
Black crow, you caw across the snow
And mock the tendrils as they early grow
Then flap your wings in spectral flight
And forever fade into the night

BIRDS AND BULLETS

Birds like darts shoot through the sky
Black bullets tear through blackest earth
Scholars in towers question why
The universe was given birth
Where armies of earth are dust of stars
That turn black holes in deepening sky
Eclipsing all man's prison bars
In the whispering ocean's questionings why
Where falling leaves are dust and arrows
The negligence of a crimson moon
When all are remembered like dust and sparrows
When our faded leaves are endless strewn

THE GRAVEDIGGER

She comes to me in visions
Kneeling beside my windy grave
I dig for all the past and future
Generations of the jasper tide
The emerald light she cusps within her hand
Illumines obsidian wings
Hovering over our gaping earth
Where she smiles with green of primal springs
Mocking screams of the buzzard's death
Where the songs of time are faintly heard
Like echoes of blackbirds on a storm

MEMENTO MORI

Today, when ownership of skulls
Is banned by democratic law,
A cup of plainest dust will do
To look on death with awe.

THE GEODE

The perimeter is etched with hardest minerals
With a center of mist and cloud
Which spiral in wilderness of starkest world
Ghostly specters of black and white
Where there is no respite from mysteries unfurled
Through clouds of ancient thunderbolt
As electrons spray within the ancient sphere
To capture flickering fear of millionth year
Of man still in his cave
Of painted orange deer on wall of firelight
Which gathers smoke in blackening background
From which unveils the electric light bulb
To darken the cave with sterile light
As clouds rekindle
In an uncracked geode...

THE NORDIC FUNERAL PYRE

Only through the narrows of the ancient woods
Could shadowed birds flow as worlds of raging floods
Beyond our borders of tumbling autumn leaves
Where flocks of blackbirds sing what river grieves
Only blackest flight could tell of flint that yearns
When fire of rock still spells what river churns
In death of flint through ancient coral spark
In untold turning's drifting bark
On the funeral pyre of man's mortality
Set adrift on waves of eternity

THE FIREFLY

All twinkling is the lightning bug
And kindling in his summer night
When all the world is slumbering snug
Only then begins his flight

Into the fiery flickering night
Of dark and cosmic gold
Of bonfires lifting crackling light
Above a world in stories told

With all of mankind growing old
Beneath the gloom of forest trees
When crackling bark all sparkling bold
The sweeping wind the spirit frees

THE EMPTY COFFIN

No one was buried on that ancient day
When endless leaves of autumn blew
Through winds of time where eons fray
With shifting sands our only clue

That mysteries are stillest skies of blue
When wise men still their riddles say
When all the birds of springtime flew
As gulls cast shadows across the windy bay

For time for no man can delay
When all the ocean shells ring true
In ancient whispers of time's decay
Where fading leaves the years still rue

Through windswept skies of endless blue
Where songs of time cannot unsay
The whispering sands alone are true
Where time through empty skies will fray

DIGGERS OF WELLS

Man has always been a digger of wells
Finding waters of life in Adam's dust
Geologic eons beneath ocean swells
Where Archimedes' lever turns to rust

Like children, men have played on layers of dirt
Drifting sands that sift in desert's clime
Like waves of Trojan spears the shores once skirt
Beneath the fading mysteries of time

For a long time, the Trojans were but myth
And men of Crete were lost beneath the seas
The men of Argos drowned within a fifth
As modern men down mountains scaled on skis

But in ancient childhood's wonder men dug deep
To resurrect all heroes Homer told
And brought to life the memories earth would keep
Of dinosaurs beyond our Hector bold

For man is just two hundred thousand years
But millions of years the dinosaurs did roam
And never could have fathomed human fears
Where ocean waves have crashed on desert loam

THE DIAMOND AND THE RAFT

The raft cuts through the ancient river
As the diamond cuts though all of time
Where eternity is forgotten sliver
That hinges on the turning dime
But is it crime to number stars
And question science of galaxies
When mankind fights in numbered wars
Forgetting eternal silence frees
We do not know the mountain snow
Erupting from earth in lattice structures
Like diamond facets the stars will show
When time and the cosmos ruptures
But only music can fathom the sliver
Where eternity and time are one
Like diamond starlight on ancient river
Where human freedom in the end light's won

CITIES OF GOLD

We will not bear the gathering sound
Outside, of sand from the desert,
Where still the ancient sunlight stares
Like Gold we did desert.

Across the marble streets it pelts,
Rolls off, and gathers into streams,
Whispering round the corners
Of the mazes of our modern dreams.

We stare amazed at gadgets we
Have made, idle idols,
We thought we caught the thunderbolt
Of God, though we are dulled

In sense and thought. We thought
Men's factories could turn plastic gold,
Not charms that char in Sinai's heat,
Black forgeries we mistook for God.

And so we gaze on sands that sift
Like streams through an ancient clock,
Common specks that mark our time
Which drift before an ageless Rock.

We watch as the desert grows
Into the cities we become,
Whose shadows are its citizens
That past the seconds flit and run.

Our cities of gold betray true rust,
Not like that Gold which was our God,
Uprooted, and in Babel's mold,
As barren breath in earthen clods.

And still the endless sunlight stares,
Great circle of eternal Gold,
At sifting of the gathering sands
Where desert winds grow bold.

THE CEMETERY TREE

In winter the cemetery tree
Drops its final autumn leaves
Like pantomimes of society
Which spring revives as stardust grieves

Gold to green, and green to gold
Like fog will spread across our minds
The cemetery tree has nightly told
What patterned snows the cold unbinds

We cannot capture granite dust
Chiseled from forgotten names
When clockwork chimes still turn to rust
In quenching of all mortal flames

And still the cemetery tree stands tall
Above our mortal fleeting graves
When outstretched arms across will gall
The barrenness of ocean waves

CHERUBIM SWORD

And is my fading life worth his
Where the ancient serpent still does hiss
In no man's land of serpentine sand
Where ocean voyagers still must strand
I saw the webs in ancient dark
With spiders caught in centers stark
I could not fathom gossamer's dew
Where men of virtue still stood few
Caught in webs of fading dark
When coyotes send their eerie bark
Like cacophony of swirling sand
Of ancient deserts of ancient man
Through hourglass of swirling time
Where beating heart still measures crime
I could not stand on head of pin
Where angels fathomed human sin
Since I was dust, and they were not
In the severed Gordian knot

BLACK FLOWERS

Why must black flowers bloom in sun
As roses drip all blood of life begun
Color TVs turn to black and white
As ghosts of truth only ghosts can write
Shadows flicker across the sandy shore
Where hope of Homer is no more
Raining spears against all skies
The sinking futile man in deafening cries
Bronze age slithering into iron AI age
Foretold by desert's blinding sage
Blackest flowers bloom in Adam's gaze
Through the Cretan Minotaur's maze
Born of Daedalus, like the one
Who flew into the only burning sun
Where waxen wings still melt into the sea
To prove that man from death cannot be free

HECATE

As you move through your four directions
Beware of her who stares at three
With stone-cold eyes of fixity
Which every mortal season shuns.

Beware of crossroads: her black birds are free,
And vacant are the eyes where dark blood runs,
Hectic streaks with no directions
Across the three-faced Hecate.

HURRICANE LAND

Winds scream across the island sands
Waves break in ever surging bands
A cry breaks from seagull's endless strength
Obsidian eyes stare at endless length
Of destruction where roofs are turned to ships
Where electric cable in sparkles whips
To harry men through the ocean's roar
Where homes of their world are nevermore
And all becomes the endless ocean's deep
Where cracking vessels hopes no longer keep
Where children in slashing rains still weep
And steel their hearts against a fatal beauty
Where to leave such land becomes their sacred duty

LOOKING INTO THE SEA

I cannot look into the sea too long
As I used to do in my faded youth.
Its waves wash over sands where shells belong,
Which long ago whispered ancient truth.
I do not care to look on crashing waves
Which hiss across our desert dune
And wash away the star that paves
The spells within an ancient rune.
For ruin is the mystery of the sea
Which still remembers all the ships of yore,
Which sank beneath a hope that could not be,
Borne by faded youth before.

THE CRACKING OF THE ROUND TABLE

Mordred cackles through the crow-filled wood
As swarms of wings surround the stone where Arthur stood
In his own youth when he drew the sword from out the quake
Which awakened goldfinch and the Lady of the Lake

Who spins her sword three times in mirror of the Trinity
Whose samite hand the mystics through the mists still see
Who have seen her silver table forever round
Where children's drifts of gold in blossoms abound

But Arthur's knights still hang from winter trees
Where the crow's voice is drowned in coldest breeze
Where a stirrup in winds still slowly cuts the cord
As dying Perceval remembers the lost accord

And the cackles that the feathered crows still throw
Cannot impenetrate the heights and depths below
Where the sacred memory of the ancient dying king
Scatters the futile and the blackest thing

11

Vestiges of Eternity

MORNING TEACUP

Only birds can fly in silence true
Inside a porcelain teacup painted blue,
In meditations on a newborn day
Of each man's hopes and fancy's feathered play,
Where death beyond the border still forebodes
In stillest mountain of the silver lodes.

Yet in its stolen moment of serenity
We see how eternity shall ever be,
Beyond the borders of our temporal wares
Where cries of trading for a teacup—no one cares—
Since in endless silence bluebirds ever fly
Where none can cry where none can ever die.

THE FIRST MINERAL

Bright diamond lost within the night
First mineral formed from Big Bang's light
You are but carbon, black as night
Yet still you wield the firstborn light
More radiant far than human marriage
Of drifting dust in horse-drawn carriage
Where dust returns to dust in age
As old black earth turned darkest sage
But still you gleam through all man's years
Outliving childhood's hopes and fears
A harder thing than falling tears
Eternal crystal birthing seers

RUINS ON A SEA CLIFF IN IRELAND

Shadows still sweep the whitened stones
Of a sunlit church that looked across the seas.
The blinding sunsets across these ancient ruins
Still spell the names of forgotten bones.

The seabirds in their shadowy flight
Forever sweep these crumbling stones,
Where dust of man the spirit frees
To tell eternal light.

Do not forget that you are in
That language of archaic flight
Where the Word of God mankind atoned,
Scattering shadows of the ancient night.

HY-BRASIL

There is an island in the unknown sea,
West of Ireland where all mysteries be.
None can find it, so they say,
When waterspouts with spirits play,
Then was Hy-Brasil on every mappèd world.
Like spinning tops by children twirled,
Found near corners of the sea and land,
Calling across the roaring ocean strand
We knew that island. Upon it, rabbits black
Like shadows leap where mortal memories stack,
When ancient waves beneath the moonlight shone
And strange magician dwelt in tower of stone.

MISTS OF IRELAND

From the wells beneath the hazelwood
The poets of Ireland's hills would drink
Where the sun above the plow once stood
While worlds beneath the waves would sink
Since only there in the misty glance
Of woods beyond the moonlit plain
Did the elves in secret circles dance
Beyond the spells of mortal pain
For the ancient wood of Adam's fall
Is cold and dark and dank
But the trees of frosted leaves grow tall
Where morning sunlight winter drank
In spells of fairy crystal blooms
That light the dark of a dying race
Like trails of robes cross desert dunes
Where all man's journeys sands retrace
In the hourglass of crimson time
Where all our hours are turned to dust
Where elves through frozen leaves still chime
As deathless spirits must
Where leaves do jangle in winter's wind
Like corpses hung from ancient trees
Where melodies the elven voices send
Where the sylvan message frees

REMBRANDT

His dark forever pierces light
Where light forever pierces dark
In murky rays of soundless night
That cross all transverse rays of light

Until we finally see the dark
And shudder 'neath a winter light
Where dark's more deep than human fright
In light beyond all mortal sight

PRAYER FOR A DYING GIRL

How strange to bring our sister dear
To this ancient whispering shore,
Where the silent bark approaches near
To take her to the other shore.

How strange that all the Fates decree
That innocents must part so soon,
That forfeiting this world to see
Be strictest cost for Heaven's boon.

And strange that whispering sea
Should be so near throughout our year,
Deeper than mortal life can be,
The endless Being of Eternity.

O Shore to be a shore no more,
Will to be Air replete with Light,
Whispering Spirit of the Sun before
Proceeding from the Fountain's might.

O Origin and End decreed
To reach beyond our phonetic sign,
Hear the prayer of the whispering reed:
Let the Rose in Heaven shine.

FOREST SANCTUARY

You lead us to your haunts, wild wood,
What would you teach us here,
Away from the wide, wide world
Where the world would not draw near?

What's in your silence, silent wood,
So vast yet ever near,
Where autumn leaves can sometimes drink
From springs still running clear?

What's in your darkness, hidden wood,
What mystery shining clear,
That shuns the glamorous glittering
That the world still holds too dear?

Where do your roots sink, deepest wood,
So deep in the turning sphere,
Which no man knows while still revolves
His life of hope and fear?

What's heard in your whispering leaves
By the wandering, listening ear,
Held in stillness in the spinning world
Where your mystery it will hear?

One day we leave this silent wood:
Its woven branches disappear,
When we walk beneath the silent sky
Where the endless stars appear.

ON THE DEATH OF AN INFANT

Brief messenger from another world
Who strayed into our realm of death
In time, when snows are softly swirled
By God's Eternal Breath.

Baby's breath that whispered endless Life,
You hold the mystery of our fading world
Where you did not know of time's brief strife,
When snows are softly swirled.

WATERFALLS

Endlessly falling through the universe
These cataracts of being,
Where now in wingèd flight the spirits
The Face of God are seeing

THE POPULAR PRESS

Beware the popular press
And its world in glittering dress;
Beware the spectral night
Mocking eternal Light.

Hold fast to ancient Gold
That mocks all fools of old;
Hold fast to eternal Light
Dispersing demons of night.

BESIDE THE STREAM

Let all be still beside that stream
Where only little children dream,
Where only falling leaves can drift,
Where gold and red in winds still sift.

For all the greens of springs have passed
And worlds are shown to never last;
Our world was first a burning sphere
Where light through clouds could not appear.

For when magmatic earth had cooled
Its black basaltic rocks then ruled,
And when its cooling vapors rained,
A thousand years their mist remained.

Let all be still beside that Breath
Which blows across both life and death,
Where Light on childhood's faded streams
A child's reflections still redeems.

ANCESTORS

We watched them journey across the snow
Beneath the ancient winter Tree,
Whose leaves are flown in bitter winds so free
Across the whispering waves below

For only when we knew them could we know
That timeless call of mystery,
What was to be must soon forever be
Lost in winter winds that blow

ACROBATS

In the circuses we watched them swinging
In our childhood between our birth and death
The fragile plots of earth, horizons singing
Where mankind's mirth is fading breath

And so they swung up into sky
The only cusp twixt earth and sea
Like falling angels hovering by
In fading time, and man's eternity

THE CALL OF ANAXAGORAS

It was heard so long ago, that call
On a now forgotten night,
Above a fragrant forest mist
That softly glowed in cosmic light.

Above the waters clear and cold,
And through the solemn forest air,
As stars reflected all around
The call was echoed everywhere.

But light's reflections could not stir
Men's souls unto their very depth,
They could not stir that starry mix
Where mirrored souls drew deeper breath.

Where light's reflections are not light
But fading waters black and cold,
And endless atoms endless spun
And not the Light of God of old.

For it appears within our soul,
Beneath the depths of all we see,
Before bright angels or their stars,
'Tis Mind that made all things that be.

All things that be within that night
When first was heard that starry call
From out eternity's abyss,
The One who fashioned each and all.

WALK ALONG THE BEACH

Since childhood I watched them hand in hand
Strange mysteries I could not understand
Of flickering specters gliding into sand
Like dust storms between the sky and land.

Beneath the cosmos I could not cry
As shadows passed us by and by
More ancient than the Serpent's lie
As sand and star will ratify.

III

Modernity's Negation

MARRIED LESBIANS

And what is beyond man's death, my child
While the sickle's sheathed where the bloom grew
    wild,
Neglecting how all the stars shone mild
Before the vernal moon was strange defiled.

A cry of rage to reach this beauteous moon
Falls silent on a world that died too soon,
And so transmutes into the mournful tune
Of ghostly winds across a barren dune.

"TO WHICH THE YEAR DID SUMMON US IN HIS DELIGHTFUL ROUND"

That was Wordsworth, whose frost still clings to tree
Which Hubble telescope from ignorance will free
Where the universe is thirteen billion years old
As Aristotle, in obscurity, foretold

Where the microcosm man forever stands
And skates across the ice and empty sands
When the universe is old as ancient Tree
Which fixes all directions wise men see

From the pole-star's light of countless billion years
Of distance where the child still throws his fears
In the skipping rock across unruffled lake
Where the Mind that made the stars is on the Stake

As the sheep in forgotten pasture quietly bleats
While a billion years of cosmic wind still fleets
Through endless trillion galaxies of stars
Where only one man, thirty-three, can reconcile all wars

THE ANADARKO

Being from Oklahoma
I have known the Anadarko
A typist's corruption of the Nadaco
Affiliated with the Caddo,
Whose forgotten word means
"The bumblebee place."
I have known that place
Being from Oklahoma
Where one cannot predict the bees
But can predict the yellow sunset
Over black forgotten swamps
That through all eons
Became our blackest gold
From Philbrook to Skelly★
Who died by spilling blackest blood
In pooling red of sunset.

★ Philbrook and Skelley were among the most prominent oilmen when Tulsa was dubbed "The Oil Capital of the World." Philbrook built a truly enormous mansion in Tulsa, designed in classical Italian style, with the most splendid garden in Oklahoma. I grew up visiting the museum it was turned into, which houses many famous paintings, an important part of my childhood formation. —WD

CULTURE OF DEATH

Ours is the culture of death,
Stifled as the child's breath,
Barren as the realm of life
With murder running rife.

Our children do not run,
They die in life begun,
But we hear their ghostly breath
In desert winds of death.

STRANGE CONFUSION

It can't be male or female,
Or female or male,
For the doctor makes another
Our sister and our brother.

INDUSTRIALISTS

These businessmen move metal for caviar
And do not question the things that are:
In Heaven and in human hands of dust
That blow away as human spirits must.

MEDIEVAL ANGEL

On sheepskin can its face still radiate gold,
Its wings still waft in censer's ember red,
But our museums cannot sense or hold
The glory that has long ago been shed.

THE ARCHAEOLOGIST'S DILEMMA

The archaeologist did not hear the wood-elves sing
When trees dew-laden wept on corpse of king
Whose withering flesh too soon would feed their leaves,
Flickering in sunlight, where no mortal grieves.

Pale scientific hands will never grasp a sword
Held high above the rush of enemy horde,
Against the only light the world has ever known
Of the brave man forgotten where his spirit's flown.

OF JETS AND LONGSHIPS

Today we cross the Atlantic by jet
Tended by friendly stewardesses
Bestowing drinks and crispy crackers.
Intercoms soothe in friendly tones
And trays deploy with a simple latch.

Not so the Vikings, not so would they traverse
The Endless, through its silver sleeting drops
That fell in starkest curtains 'cross the steeps,
Crest on crest of daunting watery mountains
Into the unknown Void.

THE NEWS CYCLE

Can you look into the ancient storm
That towers around us without form,
In deepest black, and whitest light,
In thunderbolt that shatters sight?

When all creation's dust explodes
In darkest cloud the sky forebodes,
Can you peer into the pregnant pause
When time is prey to media's claws?

Bombs of hell, of chaos round
Shred the skies from stars to ground,
And who still hears the Child's breath
Whose Word still scatters shades of death?

Or who can hear the creaking bloom
Of twittering branches through the gloom,
Where trillion blades of grasses breach
Man's darkness as the sun they reach?

And who now hears the silver stars
Sing of heroes behind steel bars,
And who will scry the empty sky
When little children ask us why?

DISTINCTIONS

Even "though" is almost spelled like "thought,"
Where thoughts are bound by words,
But thoughts by things when world was wrought
Or separate feathers in our flock of birds
Cacophony of all our scatterings
At the beginnings of the biggest bang,
And all our fleeings from the center of things
Down to the politician's dead harangue
And do not cringe before the flickering screen
Of talking heads where all things do not seem
When a cosmos helter-skelter seems to careen
But a gymnast dances miracles on wooden beam
In a world where freedom still is air
And all is lovely in the morning dream
When the crippled man can climb the ancient stair

CHILDREN'S HANDS

Cotton was too white in black hands
When soil was black and clouds were white
In northern factories soot blackened hands
Of white children whose hopes were vanished quite
In twelve-hour workdays where whistle blew their brains
Into oblivion's smog, and tumbling sands
Of receding surf returning to the abyss
Where land of children with same-colored hands
First heard in the garden the Serpent's hiss
While children of today watch man's steel cranes

PRESCIENCE

"What shadows we are, and what shadows we pursue,"
Said Edmund Burke,
While now the shadows round us lurk,
While men of light now number few.

FIDDLESTICKS!

"Fiddlesticks!" is in steep decline,
Its sense of common sense;
To nonsense must we now incline
And elders passing hence.

ARACHNE

She wove her cloth of cunning spell
Within her starry mirror,
The sea of Heaven's sins to tell
Till Heaven spoke much clearer.

And still today she weaves her web
To catch the fishes of the sea,
Within her noose—the ancient fib
That God could evil be.

DECLARATION OF INDEPENDENCE

Children wave their sparklers
In circles of light
As all the stars of Heaven
Orbit through night.

According to their natural law
The stars and children glow,
But men now trample
This natural law below.

OUR GREY CONFUSION

It can't be black and white,
It can't be white and black;
Confusion is our right
That hangs upon a tack.

For now the mother hen
Can be the falcon grey,
As even little children
Can be their mother's prey.

THE JOKER AND HIS MINIONS

As we stand in the cemetery
Numb beneath the winter sun
We hear cold winds through barren oaks
Which wreathe through ancient memories
Of mountains, seas, and sky.
All is silent, still, and holy
In the deep finality of death
Where all of human life's a flicker
Of the final golden autumn leaf.

Suddenly there appear
Clowns on unicycles
With painted faces and jeering grins
The Joker and his motley gang of fools
Scattering our solemn group
Overturning all that is sacred and silent
As they spraypaint tombs of granite with orange
And cackle like death's lord—
A man in white and his scarlet troupe
Rising up from Hell.

A DEMOCRAT MEETS A DEMAGOGUE

Do not look into Medusa's eyes
Or snakes that swim in garden streams
Like locks of hair of fading lies,
Abortion's nightmare turned to dreams

They slither away beneath the stars
That mark the days of all mankind
Where souls are lost in endless wars
When crimson chalice Arthur cannot find

For selfish slaves choose knife's revolt
Which slashes the human forest wide.
The witch has crowned the ancient dolt,
Heckler sits by Heretic's side.

THE DEMON BEGGAR

"Can you spare me a simple coin?"
 Begged the beggar at the gate of Rome,
"That a million souls can still purloin,
 Cast forever from out their Home?"

"Make sure it bears our witch's stamp,
 Pachamama of the ancient days,
 Where men on children's corpses tramp
 Which now forever become our ways."

"For convenience sake toss it in my mouth,
 Then watch it become a bubbling volcano
 That shrine of forgotten idols in the south
 Where demons helpless children throw."

TURN AWAY

Do not mind the fading world,
This "post-Christian earth,"
Where all the temporal skies are whirled
By Christ's Eternal Birth.

Spare not a minute for the minnow
In his whirlpool of the sea,
Whose ripples cannot flow
Across eternity.

ETERNITY'S ON THE VERGE

Eternity's on the verge:
Is everything we touch in time—
Where past and present merge—
An arising from evolutionary slime?

Oh, do not look behind your back
Like fated ancient Orpheus
Where wave on wave of oceans stack
To drown the old Greek chorus.

No: all arose from oceans (they say),
Great androids from a cosmic dust.
When threads of time begin to fray,
The world shall splatter, core to crust,
In a final cosmic ray.

All, for them, is progress:
Developing technology must
Obliterate what the poets say.

MAYDAY, MAYDAY

I still remember that day in a small plane
Strange engine whose wings are made to fly
Forever, like birds of any sky,
Of every heaven, without mortal pain.

I have heard the solemn seabirds cry
As they dart into the oceans' shield
When I learned to run through open field
In lost horizons of unceilinged sky.

From a burning carcass whose fire I wield
I stole the fire from out the somber sky
When a child, I could not cry
As I watched how time to death must yield.

IV

Redemption's Mystery

RENUNCIATION

The voice of the renunciation
Of all the things of time
The angel spoke, at the Annunciation
And cleansed the world of crime

And then was our world awoken
To desert stars and Heaven's clime,
The image strewn, through centuries broken,
Recollected in its Paradigm

THE WHEEL

Did past or present invent the wheel?
We think it neither, since it was there
When the cosmos first began to clink
Through alleys of time, from out nowhere.

The turning cosmos has many spokes
Which radiate from a single point,
The splinters of a single Tree
Whose chrisms kings and priests anoint.

For moderns to regain this point
They first must relearn to go nowhere,
Being still within the One
Whose Being's always everywhere.

For the whirling of the many spokes
Makes firelight in a mirror,
The constellated hopes and fears
That shimmer in a single Tear.

And rivers down the byways
And corridors of forgotten time
Still flow from springs of innocence
To wash our world of its ancient crime.

VERBUM EFFICIT

The only human words
To survive the winds of time
Are ink on wood,
Flecks of breath
Of the Only-Begotten Word.

THE WOODS OF BETHLEHEM

Eyes that stare through hollowed wood
Our vanished place we dare not venture through
Where swirling witches moonlight wooed
Where collars white kept track of two and two
Since vanished is the curtain shrouding Mars
Where eyes of elves have always seen too far
Past haunting of the ocean's sandy bars
Where every sunken ship has died beneath the star
Of Bethlehem that sank our mortal world
When all the leaves of autumn slowly swirled
When the cosmos by a Child was twirled
And shadows to the outer darkness hurled

VIETNAM

Wriggling fingers from man's abyss
We view them from the gutters nigh
In trees we hear the serpent's hiss
From tongues unfurled beneath the sky
And dare not do and dare not die
When flames against the skies are hurled
When Marxist flags are raised on high
When deathless spirit is denied
For no man can reach the why
Though every mortal man has tried
And bravest man shall heave a sigh
Remembering Christ for the Commie died

MOUNT ATHOS

Since we should breathe with both our lungs
But never speak divided tongues,
Let's praise the hoary Athos men
Who find a paradise again.

On canes, in painful weariness,
They bear their cross, they learn to bless,
In realms of purest spirit lifted,
Their sins in sieves of grace are sifted.

They are His Body then, as we,
Though this we cannot always see,
As they are gazing still transfixed
Where God and time have meetly mixed

Upon the forest Cross, above
The deepening cobalt sea of love
That Homer saw but could not know,
Where wreathing thorns and roses grow.

THE ANCIENT CHOIR

All the fled and fleeting strands of time
Weave together in a greater rhyme
Where small and larger feet on ocean strand
Are gathered in the fading cosmic sand
Into a music raging in the surf
Across the slickness of our glassy turf
Which mirrors flickering hope of whitest stars
Echoing depths beyond the sandy bars
Where death is drowned within unfathomed deep
In promises the faithful stars still keep
Where waters 'gainst the perilous rocks still ram
In memory of the only murdered Lamb

ST. THÉRÈSE IN THE PANTHEON

Silently, in the Pantheon
On summer's Pentecost
Rose petals drift upon
The ground where Rome was lost.

Silently in the autumn field
Where sunlit grains are shorn
Reddest rains of roses yield
The children that are born.

THORNS AND DIAMONDS

A flock of roses
Decks the circled thorn,
As crowns of gold are forged
Where sheep are shorn.

Blacksmith of the diamond
How could you know,
That dust of carbon
Could most radiant glow?

THE MAYFLY

For 2,000 years mankind has lived
In the silent wake of eternity
The vertical pole still reaching the utmost star
Whose ripples roll forever,
About which time has slowly turned,
Intersecting an ancient piece of wood
Taken from a carbon tree
Whose name very few remember.

For man like a mayfly
Is scorched in electric light
Held to a weathered pole
By the fishing dock
And mirroring lake in the dark,
Where the creaking cosmos,
Gathering waters of life,
Sustains the endless journey
That never was horizontal
But Dark and Light
Day and Night,
The only span of the mayfly.

BLIND DUST

O swirling gas of endless carbon
You could not witness history pass
When Spirit joined with dust of Adam
To undo atoms' one trespass.

THE MASS OF MASS...

...weighs upon the universe
And all the mattered matter
And infinity that has not matter
The Word that mirrors God the Father
Reflecting as the silent Dove
Speaking all that is
In creation and in God above,
Of a universe that is,
And endless worlds that might have been,
Descends within the Eucharist.

HERETIC'S DILEMMA

I had a friend, who with his knowledge-hoard
Could argue spots off every leopard.
He argued that the Word is only sword
And not a silent Shepherd.
He stood for iron chains and fiery stake
That bear resemblance to unsheathed claws,
And eyes with mortal pain and fear awake
When furry leg is caught in biting jaws.
A second friend's response, in moonlit waves,
Surpassed dark knowledge of all fallen flesh
For him, God's grace a truer path still paves,
Where Mercy's everlasting oceans mesh.

ON THE SHEDDING OF BLOOD

Christ's Blood was not shed for those who followed Him
That they might in His name shed further blood
But in His desert, they might raise their hymn
Remembering whitest dove beyond red Flood

Which flows through ancient Sacraments from skies
To cover a world in mercy, which transcends
And drowns salt tears of pitiful mortal cries
Where Blood of Christ turns hearts as hope ascends

IN THE FULLNESS OF TIME

When Plato's Forms drew mortal eyes
Unto the distant skies,
The Word descended from those skies
To Flesh immortalize.

AN INNOCENT CROSS

A cross of silence
A loss of noise
A sunlit desert
Are childhood's toys

EDEN AND ATLANTIS

There are two eternal poles
The positive and negative charge
The earthworm and wormholes
The current and anchorless empty barge

There's God and man, thunderbolt, and sand
Spirit of atoms, angels, and Adam
Spectral zircons in sedimentary band
In Australian hills where there is no dam

To stop the flood of Hadean magma
That flows throughout our ocean world
Where deep time history is the stigma
To those in mayfly currents swirled

For mankind fears those eyes that look in wells
That sink beneath the covers of all skies
They fear the scarab which in desert dwells
And blind Tiresias who discovers lies

For there is only Adam and zircon
The Spirit of all in windblown rust
Luciferian dust, or the God we look upon
In awe, in spirit, and in trust

EGYPTIAN HIEROGLYPHS

Egyptian hieroglyphs have buried our world
In age-old sands beneath the startled sun,
In fragments of mysteries on scrolls unfurled
Beneath the moon when our world was young.

I know of answers to forgotten riddles old:
When the myth of man—four, two, and three legged—
Was the later one, the accretion Sophocles then told,
While by the Nile River moon-day man still begged.

I know the meaning of the lion's sandy mane
Between pharaonic face and endless skies,
Whose four-limbed mystery kept his people sane
Beside the desert winds that whisper lies.

Truly: cobalt sky is still the sacred pool
Where ancient Adam bathes through all of time,
Where Adonai still makes his foes a footstool,
Though scientists spell eons out of slime.

For the Emerald Tablet told of the Ancient One
In whom everything returns where it began,
The mixture of Thoth and Hermes light has won,
When beneath the dying sun old Adam ran.

I catch the light that sinks beneath the pyramids,
Whose earthly turnings turn to desert winds,
Where the sphinx's eyes still stare beneath their lids
At the sun whose ancient atoms Adam rends.

OUR PASSING

O let us pass like the evening wind
Through softly whispering grass,
Near rippling waters of a fading light
Where soon the stars will circle past.

Our souls must cross through fleshly grass
Past borders of an evening light,
To waken wonder beyond our sin
Where Heaven's stars still beckon bright.

O let us fade with each passing day
Whose shadows lengthen into our past,
And hear what the rippling stars will say
By margins of the fading grass.

For when our days and yesterdays
Are joined in the parting light,
We hear what the whispering winds will say
To flesh in the cosmic night.

When Flesh of Christ has silent passed
Through fields of the evening light,
And all the circling stars at last
Give birth to the Morning Light.

WONDER'S DEPTHS

Wonder is deeper
Than our abysses of sorrow
Or despair,
Is deeper than the pit of death
Being the pith of gold
Of silver stars
That twinkle through
Our blackest canopies
That tinge all greens
Of dripping leaves of spring
Foretelling all
Our drifts of wind
Cross the endless banks of snow
Where final crimson leaves will fall
To consecrate our whitest death
Like a teardrop,
Or blood drip
Spilling down the Face of Christ
Of the ancient Tree
Of our endless leaves
Of crimson before the whitest cold
That sprinkles all the corridors
Of all our schools and hospitals,
And hospitality balls
Whose ghosts still echo
Across the forgotten past.

THE SPELL OF HERACLITUS

Endless waters stream
Over river rocks that echo
The stars beyond man's reach
In his eternal form
As he places his foot
In the riverbed
That can never be the same
Twice in the moments of time
Where his foot drifts away
Into deserts of windswept dust
In sands and wings
Of fading sparrows
Whose flickering atoms
Are Adam's hopes
Of deserts to atone
The ancient sun
That sifts all black and white
Like drift of dice
On greenest fields of felt,
Of rolling ships
Whose prows are pointed nowhere
But the rolling waves of chaos
Save the starlight
That stills the darkening waters
As rivers nourish the sparkling fields
Of speckled starlings
Whirled by the scarecrow
Where the windvane spins
In endless storms

DIVINE TORNADO

Did you see the Holy Dove
Descend upon our human land?
There he stood like wind from above
Crumbling flesh to desert sand
To gather into eternal love.

AN ARTHURIAN MYSTERY

Look outside: all that was best of green is turning gold,
When we see the Green Knight hasten to Camelot,
With Christ's eternal golden shield, to spar with
    Adam old
Warning how the world's spring must rot.

Though its spring will rot, this world that's been
Melting in the eternal breath of God
Will rise again to primal place of green
Where angels, elves, and men have trod.

THE BELL

Slumbering I dreamt I heard a bell,
And waking I asked this dream to tell
All that it could of starry skies
Where hopes of a fading world arise.

Then softly tolled the end of death,
That bell of hope through final breath,
In gentle tones of beckoning stars
Beyond this world's wrought prison bars.

MARY OF THE CIRCLING STARS

Mary, who wove an endless crown of thorns
In stillest moment of her consent,
With threadless circle's eternity
Our history has rent.

Mary, whose circling golden stars
Still wave in Europe's flags of blue,
Above a murk of fading Faith
In words of splendor, free and true.

All threads of nations' histories fray
Beneath that sky of fadeless blue,
Of deep abyss that wise men say
Once spoke the only Word that's True.

LADY OF THE SEA

Her flowing robes are billowing
Across the quiet sea,
Where all the stars are glowing
In rolling mists stands she,
Silently gazing on the Light
Gathered in Heaven's ancient mirror
That reached across the deepest night
Where rose a Cross Her Son once bore.

FINAL BREATH

A gust of wind will carry us beyond
A world of clattering falling leaves.

Here, spirit in fallen flesh does not belong,
Where sand through endless desert sieves
The whisperings of our mortal song.

There, a fading breath which fills all sails
Passes to where gathering shadows throng.

Now only a prayer to Mary still avails.

V

The Seasons' Wheel

TREE FROG

The tree frog on the windowpane
Is held upon a vision
Of black cloud's impending rain,
Caught in indecision.

Unaware of supervision
We see his heartbeat through the rain;
Midst art and nature, strange division
We see within the windowpane.

THE CHURCH DOOR

Past the churchyard trembling children go
Beneath the merry light of skies too blue
The red flies zig-zag to and fro
Before the church door fashioned true
Its woven fibrous willow wood
Are children's hairs of golden hue
Forgotten tree that once had stood
Beneath the skies that sparrows knew
The winds still whisper through the willow leaves
In all the spring light's glistening skew
Before the time when winter grieves
In whispering skies so still and blue

FOREST IN RAIN

Enter not this lonely grove — unless you dare
Your solemn heart from fallen world to tear,
And steal away from all its fleshly fears
In falling rain of Heaven's tears.

FIREWORKS

A shooting star across the pond
Kaboom—
Becomes a thousand shrieking stars,
Zings, and swiftly buzzing swirls
Mirrored in the water's black.
Then, when things have settled in the stars,
The ribbits of the frogs resume.

THE SPECTRAL HORSEMAN

The spectral horseman rides across the moon
Surrounded by dark seas of endless stars
His image casts a light like brightest noon
His piercing eyes are blood of reddest Mars

He carries his jack-o'-lantern through the skies
Whose candled jeers drip spells throughout the night
He cackles as he hears the hollow cries
Of flickering souls now lost in mortal fright

And so he shows each man what fills his head
The tallow pillar's hope throughout the year
As we carve a harvest pumpkin in our stead
Whose slanted burning eyes can't shed a tear

HARVEST OF THE LEAVES

See how all the citizens
Gather the crumbling leaves
Gently falling in fading color
To where the winter grieves

See how all the citizens
Process to the destined field
Carrying baskets filled
With what the trees could yield

See how all the citizens
Await their winter breeze
To cast into the heavens
The harvest of the leaves

THE CELTIC MYSTERY

We see an ancient circle in the spring
Of whitest mushrooms of the fairy ring,
Of troubled rains that yesterdays still bring
To all the circling mysteries that sing.

We heard its ancient call in autumn bright
Of fading falling leaves of human blight,
Where never ends the solemn southern flight
Of wingèd spirits fleeing golden light.

It still was heard in winter's faded gold
Where all of ancient truth is finally told,
When all the fairies die in days of old
While leaving final words in dark and cold.

For then we finally hear them faintly sing
Of truths that only faded leaves can bring,
Of the primrose, our harbinger of spring
And the Cross road, that links the endless ring.

LEAVES IN THE NIGHT

What do they sing, the autumn leaves
Beneath the starry night,
The leaves that drift in cosmic winds
With gold's eternal light?

They whisper ever quietly
Of worlds adrift in wind
And how the ancient cosmos too
Will vanish in the end.

CHILDREN IN AUTUMN

These trees that reach the skies
Are books to children's eyes;
The chilly autumn brook
Their leaves of ruby took.

That circle of blue sky
In empty branches high
Is now their only gem,
And Heaven's diadem.

The spring of emerald leaves
Are gold to him who grieves;
As every child sees
Our death is like the trees.

AUTUMN'S THE SEASON

Autumn's the season for the poet
Who dwells on cusps of dark and light,
Of flickering leaves of gold and red
Like glowing shades of morning life
That merge with streams of scarlet death.

Autumn's the season for everyman
Who cares not for the spells of reason
Which cast his stars in diagrams
But cannot see his twinkling void
Or flow of flowers fading to the dust.

Autumn's the season for the greenest leaf,
For speckled sparrow in the endless air
Forgotten on the lonely stair
But still remembered by the windy Star
Outshining the flickering of his leaves.

AUTUMN CLOUDS

Do not mind the wandering clouds of day
Where all untethered thoughts are running free
Where layered skies o'er stillest lake convey
To restive man the joy to simply be.

And do not mind the fleeting mirror
Made one with all the skies above
Where the longing deer still flees our error
That exchanges hate for proven love

And do not mind a brushwood forest hut:
Simplicity dwells in fall of autumn leaves
Where grains of wheat the scythes still cut
To gather in the weary world that grieves

THE ACORN TREE

No more my days beneath the acorn tree
When winds could tune its leaves to endless youth
Since endless green has turned to deepest red
And sings through songs of autumn's truth

ABANDONED TRAIN TRACKS

Rusted train tracks disappear into the wood
Of red and golden leaves of autumn flood,
Victorian memories in the living inferno
Where suns burn brightest where none should go

For down such paths all leaves forever fall
Where billion years the stars could call
As black they fell, turning to glittering coal
As stardust turns to sands on shifting ocean's shoal

For who could take that train where all things fade
Into a world where men must ply their metal trade
In cities which soon must turn to dust
Where blaze of autumn leaves melts all tracks of rust

THE WINTER OF US ALL

To the bones we go
To dust we flee
Where to and fro
The winds do blow,
The starry dust is you and me.

The wave upon the lake
The voice of forest round
The pines our spirits shake
Dropping needles to the ground,
The windy snows of winter's call
All glittering in the dark
Their patterns tell of each and all
Where history ends in winter stark.

But not in endless dark
Or in the solemn call
We hear around the fragrant bark
Of solemn pines that tell us all,
In endless whispering sound
That time can never take
Where snowy patterns still abound
Which endless thought did make
And endless thought sets free,
Where winter winds blow to and fro
Around that ancient winter Tree
From where the spring will grow.

FALLING SNOW

Then surely death is beautiful
Since all its signs are true,
When all its myriad messengers
The mountaintops pursue

Their silent songs were scarcely heard
In springtime's skies of blue,
Though all their endless patterns
Had told us what is true —

Of birth eternal, in a tattered world
Sprung from Spirit's hue,
When the silent Word became a Child,
To end the death we rue.

WINTER BRIDGE

I saw a winter bridge by barren tree.
It beckoned, cosmic winds still blowing free,
When all was still, save final falling leaf,
Memento of fair age of mortal grief.
We should not shun the final age of snows
When every light of Heaven brightly glows.
There is a peace beyond this fading world,
A vision's fading bridge for us unfurled
In heroes' pageantry from early years
That fortified our hearts from mortal fears,
A march of ghostly soldiers white and true
Whose voice is crashing waves of ocean blue.

THE DYING OF THE YEAR

Drip, drop, the waters fall in a darkening wood
The dying of the year where all the trees have stood
Like ranks of men against a granite wall
(The old crone cowers beneath her shawl)
Where blackest veins are human immortality
Of all forgotten runes that tell man what must be
Across our granite stones all mortals scrawl
Red-lettered leaves of fire for each and all
That splinter through all worlds like finest webs
In whispering shores where moonlight ebbs
And flows, where all the furthest stars still glow,
Where blackest branches through the skies still show
The interstitial lines that every poet mines
Like every ancient world's forgotten rhymes
Brightest runes of gold in sunset's cataract,
Where every mortal wish still fails to act
In the beauty of it all, in the harrowing of it all,
In the forest's dying of the ancient Fall.

THE ANCIENT HERMIT

Only winds in pine trees sing of solitude
Where fading human speech dissolves in platitude
When the soul's alone in endless wind
Through cosmic dark the stars their light will send
Only chickadees will sing the end of ice
When rarest men have paid the highest price
Where winter is the peak of quietude
When the ancient hermit whispers songs of gratitude

FALLING SNOWS

In the silence of the falling snows
In their patterns of infinity
The mind is wakened to what the cosmos shows
To those who know what is to be

In the kindling of the forest snows
In the fires of ice where all men see
The emptiness of circus shows
Where circling newsreels shall never be

Where the Sower in the Field still sows
His breath of snows across the sea
Where the seed into the forest grows
Where the campfire is you and me

Where we saw the falling of the Fall
Where all is all in all
In the Baby's breath in the manger's stall
Where man still heeds his pattern's call

CHRISTMAS MMXX

I play the fool, for what the hell,
I hear our world is not too well,
I look into an ancient dell
And see the demons swell.

Of eternity I cannot tell,
I cannot break the ancient spell,
But I know where the snowdrops dwell,
I heard the first Noel.

For man is spirit ethereal
Now trapped in realms material,
Who gazing round with eyes of gall
Renounces Christ for Baal.

And here I hear the demons wail
And read the blind man's craggly brail,
And watch the seeming helpless flail
And peer beyond the veil.

For human worth's what's in the scale
When man appears too lorn and frail,
Caught within the ancient tales
Where God made flesh prevails.

WINTER'S CURSE

Winter winds in howling rage
Sweep through forest branches bare
Absence of their leaves presage
Empty branches nothing care

Bleakest specters, twisting skies
In the crimson sunset glare,
Capture shrouds of chilling cries,
Glassy eyes of blackbird's stare

Winter turns another page
History's roiling, stark and spare,
As all cosmic storms engage
Emergent springs in sufferings rare,

Stubborn foliage still defies
Violent claws in bitter air
When all winter stars arise
And all branches remnants tear

A CHRISTMAS POEM

What's in your gaze of steel, my friend,
As you contemplate the depths of time,
Of length and breadth and ordained end,
That background space of Adam's crime?

Where came such thoughts of endless Light
Erupting through where time's resistance ran,
Where stillest star once shone through night
When Bethlehem did bear the Second Man?

BLOSSOMS IN THE BRIARS

See how the blossoms bloom
Into the single morning sun,
As dust on a fragrant breeze
Drifts where Adam's children run.

Censers send Ash Wednesday's clouds
Into the heavenly choirs
And foretell how rains must fall
On blossoms in the briars.

THE SWALLOW

We watch the swallow soar and sweep
Across a springtime field
And sing of where no man can weep,
Where winter's death is healed.

He builds his home of blackened earth
Beneath the ancient span,
He builds in winter's death the hearth
To spare from cold his clan.

For only when the winter's gone
He peeps from out his nest
To sing to man the springtime song
Where man can find true rest.

And when we see the fields of spring
Must blossom in their time,
The swallow rises on his wing,
Unto his native clime.

THE RED HONEYSUCKLE
Easter of Covid-19

It is the tidings of Easter Season
And all the churches are standing closed
The bounty of Christ's Blood, surpassing reason
Still cleanses the Upper Room transposed

It is the tidings of Easter Season
In all of Nature's noble robe
Her scarlet blooms recall the treason
That crowned our God, and all the globe

DUST OF LENT

The most important part of Lent
Is what all earth has spent
In its begetting of new forms
In its forgetting springtime storms

All dust returns to dust
And everything must rust
In this machine, our modern world,
Through the cosmic whirlwind whirled

The motorcades still carry men with canes
With our forgotten memory of Cain,
And women still must marry able men
Who scatter dust across our world of sin

Like desert dust that blackens in fiery sun
Strange promises that cross the men who run
Across this tiny marble of our globe
Spun through the cosmic void, an anaerobe

CHILD OF SPRING

We see the halo above the child of spring,
Thinking he knows what winter's cold will bring,
Who cannot know of blinding snows that sting
Lost on the currents of the zephyr's wing.

But he sees the halo we forgot in spring
Where winter's death still crowns a Child king,
As streaks of dark the snow-born flowers bring
Which the Garden's ancient cherubim still sing.

SAKURA

A maiden in her silk kimono—
Pink blossom on a cherry spray;
Her ivory fingers pluck the Koto
To mark a future day.

The mournful song must one day blow
Across a faded bloom,
When ghostly winds so pale and slow
Will wisp her from her room.

CLIMBING THE MAPLE TREE

In childhood I climbed the maple tree
Whose branches brushed infinity;
It weathered every natural storm
That broke across our human form.

I climbed its lightning and its storm
And the specters dusk would form;
I climbed into its golden night
Within the darkest canvas bright.

I climbed its crimson leaves of spring
Which foretell what life will bring;
I climbed its greener summer leaves
Whose loss of spring all time still grieves.

I climbed its endless falling leaves
To which each sylvan poet cleaves,
The fading orange, gold, and red
For whose sorrows God once bled.

But then I saw its winter skies
Whose beauty restless ocean sighs,
A deeper blue behind the Tree
Whose crossbeam sets God's children free.

ABOUT THE AUTHOR

Born in Tulsa, Oklahoma, William Dunn has spent much of his life in rural northeastern Oklahoma, in an area dotted with small farms and wooded lakes. His experience in these natural surroundings provides imagery for much of his writing. While attending Thomas Aquinas College in Santa Paula, California, he studied liberal arts and philosophy, and there he was received into the Roman Catholic Church. He later studied theology in Rome and Austria, along with a semester in Oxford. While studying at the International Theological Institute in Gaming, Austria, he became a student and friend of Fr. John Saward, who encouraged his interests in theology and in the traditional forms of English prosody. Dunn's essays and poems have frequently appeared in the *St. Austin Review*, edited by Joseph Pearce and Robert Asch. His first volume of verse, *Wind Among the Leaves*, was published in 2012 by Kaufmann Publishing. He currently teaches classes in philosophy, theology, and literature.

www.ingramcontent.com/pod-product-compliance
Lightning Source LLC
Chambersburg PA
CBHW030241010526
44107CB00030B/1289/J